BETTER HOMES IN AMERICA

LECTOR HOUSE PUBLIC DOMAIN WORKS

This book is a result of an effort made by Lector House towards making a contribution to the preservation and repair of original classic literature. The original text is in the public domain in the United States of America, and possibly other countries depending upon their specific copyright laws.

In an attempt to preserve, improve and recreate the original content, certain conventional norms with regard to typographical mistakes, hyphenations, punctuations and/or other related subject matters, have been corrected upon our consideration. However, few such imperfections might not have been rectified as they were inherited and preserved from the original content to maintain the authenticity and construct, relevant to the work. The work might contain a few prior copyright references as well as page references which have been retained, wherever considered relevant to the part of the construct. We believe that this work holds historical, cultural and/or intellectual importance in the literary works community, therefore despite the oddities, we accounted the work for print as a part of our continuing effort towards preservation of literary work and our contribution towards the development of the society as a whole, driven by our beliefs.

We are grateful to our readers for putting their faith in us and accepting our imperfections with regard to preservation of the historical content. We shall strive hard to meet up to the expectations to improve further to provide an enriching reading experience.

Though, we conduct extensive research in ascertaining the status of copyright before redeveloping a version of the content, in rare cases, a classic work might be incorrectly marked as not-in-copyright. In such cases, if you are the copyright holder, then kindly contact us or write to us, and we shall get back to you with an immediate course of action.

HAPPY READING!

BETTER HOMES IN AMERICA

MRS. W. B. MELONEY (MARIE MATTINGLY MELONEY)

ISBN: 978-93-5614-021-9

Published: -

LECTOR HOUSE LLP
E-MAIL: lectorpublishing@gmail.com

BETTER HOMES IN AMERICA

PLAN BOOK FOR DEMONSTRATION WEEK
OCTOBER 9 TO 14, 1922

BY

MRS. W. B. MELONEY

CONTENTS

THE WHITE HOUSE WASHINGTON

July 21, 1922.

My Dear Mrs. Meloney:

I am directed by the President to assure you of his earnest endorsement of the Better Homes Campaign which has been launched by the Advisory Council and is being carried on by representative women of America. He regards the campaign as of particular importance, because it places emphasis not only upon home ownership, which he regards as absolutely elemental in the development of the best citizenship, but upon furnishing, sanitation and equipment of the home.

The President feels that as many millions of dollars and the best minds of this generation have been devoted to improve factory conditions, the home is deserving of its share of the same intensive consideration. There are twenty millions of house-keepers in America. For them, the home is their industrial center as well as their place of abode, and it is felt that altogether too little attention has been paid to lightening the labors and bettering the working conditions of these women.

The President feels that the women, who are so successfully conducting this campaign are entitled to all consideration and recognition, and he hopes that every community in America will exhibit a model home.

Your sincerely,
Secretary to the President.

Mrs. W. B. Meloney, Sec'y., Advisory Council for Better Homes Campaign, 223 Spring Street, New York City, N. Y.

BETTER HOMES DEMONSTRATION WEEK

ADVISORY COUNCIL

CALVIN COOLIDGE, *Vice-President of the United States*

HERBERT HOOVER, *Secretary of Commerce*

HENRY C. WALLACE, *Secretary of Agriculture*

JAMES JOHN DAVIS, *Secretary of Labor*

Dr. HUGH S. CUMMING, *Surgeon-General United States Public Health Service*

Dr. JOHN JAMES TIGERT, *U. S. Commissioner of Education*

C. W. PUGSLEY, *Assistant Secretary of Agriculture*

JOHN M. GRIES, *Director Division of Building and Housing, Dept. of Commerce*

JULIUS H. BARNES, *President Chamber of Commerce of the United States*

JOHN IHLDER, *Director Housing Conditions, Chamber of Commerce of the United States*

DONN BARBER, *Fellow American Institute of Architects*

JOHN BARTON PAYNE, *Chairman Central Committee American Red Cross*

LIVINGSTON FARRAND, *Chairman National Health Council*

Mrs. THOMAS G. WINTER, *President General Federation of Women's Clubs*

MRS. LENA LAKE FORREST, *President National Federation of Business and Professional Women's Clubs*

CO-OPERATING GOVERNORS

ALASKA	SCOTT C. BONE, *Governor*
ARIZONA	THOS. E. CAMPBELL, *Governor*
ARKANSAS	T. C. McRAE, *Governor*
COLORADO	O. H. SHOUP, *Governor*
FLORIDA	CARY A. HARDEE, *Governor*
IDAHO D.	W. DAVIS, *Governor*
INDIANA	W. T. McCRAY, *Governor*
KANSAS	HENRY J. ALLEN, *Governor*
KENTUCKY	E. P. MORROW, *Governor*

MARYLAND	A. C. RITCHIE, *Governor*
MASSACHUSETTS	C. H. COX, *Governor*
MISSISSIPPILEE	M. RUSSELL, *Governor*
MISSOURI	A. M. HYDE, *Governor*
NEBRASKA	S. R. McKELVIE, *Governor*
NEVADA	E. D. BOYLE, *Governor*
OHIO	H. L. DAVIS, *Governor*
OREGON	B. W. OLCOTT, *Governor*
PENNSYLVANIA	W. C. SPROUL, *Governor*
SOUTH CAROLINA	WILSON G. HARVEY, *Governor*
SOUTH DAKOTA	W. H. McMASTER, *Governor*
TENNESSEE	ALFRED A. TAYLOR, *Governor*
UTAH	CHAS. R. MABEY, *Governor*
VERMONT	JAMES HARTNESS, *Governor*
VIRGINIA	E. L. TRINKLE, *Governor*
WYOMING	ROBERT D. CAREY, *Governor*

* * * * *

New York City Secretary, Mrs. William Brown Meloney

BETTER HOMES
BY CALVIN COOLIDGE

We spend too much time in longing for the things that are far off and too little in the enjoyment of the things that are near at hand. We live too much in dreams and too little in realities. We cherish too many impossible projects of setting worlds in order, which are bound to fail. We consider too little plans for putting our own households in order, which might easily be made to succeed. A large part of our seeming ills would be dispelled if we could but turn from the visionary to the practical. We need the influence of vision, we need the inspiring power of ideals, but all these are worthless unless they can be translated into positive actions.

The world has been through a great spiritual and moral awakening in these last few years. There are those who fear that this may all be dissipated. It will be unless it can be turned into something actual. In our own country conditions have developed which make this more than ever easy of accomplishment. It ought to be expressed not merely in official and public deeds, but in personal and private actions. It must come through a realization that the great things of life are not reserved for the enjoyment of a few, but are within the reach of all.

There are two shrines at which mankind has always worshipped, must always worship: the altar which represents religion, and the hearthstone which represents the home.

These are the product of fixed beliefs and fixed modes of living. They have not grown up by accident; they are the means, deliberate, mature, sanctified, by which the human race, in harmony with its own great nature, is developed and perfected. They are at once the source and the result of the inborn longing for what is completed, for what has that finality and security required to give to society the necessary element of stability.

The genius of America has long been directed to the construction of great highways and railroads, the erection of massive buildings for the promotion of trade and the transaction of public business. It has supplied hospitals, institutions of learning and places of religious worship. All of these are worthy of the great effort and the sustained purpose which alone has made them possible. They contribute to the general welfare of all the people, but they are all too detached, too remote; they do not make the necessary contribution of a feeling of proprietorship and ownership. They do not complete the circuit. They are for the people, but not of the people. They do not satisfy that longing which exists in every human breast to be able to say: "This is mine."

We believe in American institutions. We believe that they are justified by the light of reason, and by the result of experience. We believe in the right of self-government. We believe in the protection of the personal rights of life and liberty and the enjoyment of the rewards of industry. We believe in the right to acquire, to hold, and transmit property. We believe in all that which is represented under the general designation of a republic.

But while we hold that these principles are sound we do not claim that they have yet become fully established. We do not claim that our institutions are yet perfected.

It is of little avail to assert that there is an inherent right to own property unless there is an open opportunity that this right may be enjoyed in a fair degree by all. That which is referred to in such critical terms as capitalism cannot prevail unless it is adapted to the general requirements. Unless it be of the people it will cease to have a place under our institutions, even as slavery ceased.

It is time to demonstrate more effectively that property is of the people. It is time to transfer some of the approbation and effort that has gone into the building of public works to the building, ornamenting, and owning of private homes by the people at large—attractive, worthy, permanent homes.

Society rests on the home. It is the foundation of our institutions. Around it are gathered all the cherished memories of childhood, the accomplishments of maturity, and the consolations of age. So long as a people hold the home sacred they will be in the possession of a strength of character which it will be impossible to destroy.

Apparently the world at large, certainly our own country, is turning more and more for guidance to that wisdom born of affection which we call the intuition of woman. Her first thought is always of the home. Her first care is for its provision. As our laws and customs are improved by her influence, it is likely to be first in the direction of greater facility for acquiring, and greater security in holding a home.

Some of the fine enthusiasm which was developed by the required sacrifices of war may well find a new expression in turning towards the making of the home. It is the final answer to every challenge of the soundness of the fundamental principles of our institutions. It holds the assurance and prospect of contentment and of satisfaction.

Under present conditions any ambition of America to become a nation of home owners would be by no means impossible of fulfillment. The land is available, the materials are at hand, the necessary accumulation of credit exists, the courage, the endurance and the sacrifice of the people are not wanting. Let them begin, however slender their means, the building and perfecting of the national character by the building and adorning of a home which shall be worthy of the habitation of an American family, calm in the assurance that "the gods send thread for a web begun."

Here will be found that satisfaction which comes from possession and achievement. Here is the opportunity to express the soul in art. Here is the Sacred influence, here in the earth at our feet, around the hearthstone, which raises man to his true estate.

(Signed)
Calvin Coolidge

THE HOME AS AN INVESTMENT
BY HERBERT HOOVER

One can always safely judge of the character of a nation by its homes. For it is mainly through the hope of enjoying the ownership of a home that the latent energy of any citizenry is called forth. This universal yearning for better homes and the larger security, independence and freedom that they imply, was the aspiration that carried our pioneers westward. Since the preemption acts passed early in the last century, the United States, in its land laws, has recognized and put a premium upon this great incentive. It has stimulated the building of rural homes through the wide distribution of land under the Homestead Acts and by the distribution of credit through the Farm Loan Banks. Indeed, this desire for home ownership has, without question, stimulated more people to purposeful saving than any other factor. Saving, in the abstract, is, of course, a perfunctory process as compared with purposeful saving for a home, the possession of which may change the very physical, mental, and moral fibre of one's own children.

Now, in the main because of the diversion of our economic strength from permanent construction to manufacturing of consumable commodities during and after the war, we are short about a million homes. In cities such a shortage implies the challenge of congestion. It means that in practically every American city of more than 200,000, from 20 to 30 per cent, of the population is adversely affected, and that thousands of families are forced into unsanitary and dangerous quarters. This condition, in turn, means a large increase in rents, a throw-back in human efficiency and that unrest which inevitably results from inhibition of the primal instinct in us all for home ownership. It makes for nomads and vagrants. In rural areas it means aggravation and increase of farm tenantry on one hand, an increase of landlordism on the other hand, and general disturbance to the prosperity and contentment of rural life.

There is no incentive to thrift like the ownership of property. The man who owns his own home has a happy sense of security. He will invest his hard earned savings to improve the house he owns. He will develop it and defend it. No man ever worked for, or fought for a boarding-house.

But the appalling anomaly of a nation as prosperous as ours thwarted largely in its common yearning for better homes, is now giving way to the gratifying revival of home construction. Accordingly the time is ripe for this revival to afford an opportunity to our people to look to more homes and better ones, to better, more economical and more uniform building codes, and to universal establishment and application of zoning rules that make for the development of better towns and cities. We have the productive capacity wasted annually in the United States sufficient to raise in large measure the housing conditions of our entire people to the level that only fifty per cent, of them now enjoy. We have wastes in the building industry itself which, if constructively applied, would go a long way toward supplying better homes, so that what is needed imperatively is organized intelligence and direction. For the problem is essentially one of ways and means.

And, finally, while we are about Better Homes for America and are lending such indirect support to the movement as the Government, States, counties, communities, and patriotic individuals and organizations can rightfully give, let us have in mind not houses merely, but homes! There is a large distinction. It may have been a typesetter who confounded the two words. For, curiously, with all our American ingenuity and resourcefulness, we have overlooked the laundry and the kitchen, and thrown the bulk of our efforts in directions other than those designed to make better homes by adding to the facilities of our very habitations. If, in other words, the family is the unit of modern civilization, the home, its shelter and gathering-point, should, it would seem, warrant in its design and furnishing quite as large a share of attention as the power plant or the factory.

We believe, therefore, that in every community in which it is possible a *"Better Homes in America"* Demonstration should be planned and carried through during the week of October 9th to 14th, 1922.

(Signed)
HERBERT HOOVER

THE SECRETARY OF AGRICULTURE
WASHINGTON

July 24, 1922.

DEAR MRS. MELONEY:

Naturally I am interested in the "Better Homes in America" movement. When we consider the all powerful influence of home conditions and home atmosphere on the lives and character of our people, both young and old, surely every proper effort to improve those conditions should have the support of all good citizens.

Our people in the Department of Agriculture will be glad to advise with your committee chairmen on any matters in which they can lend assistance. Our home demonstration agents in different sections of the country can no doubt be helpful in advising as to the setting up of demonstration kitchens.

You seem to have gathered to your help the cooperation of a large number of state governors and also a number of other gentlemen who, because of their public work, can possibly contribute to the success of the campaign.

With very best wishes, I am
Sincerely yours,

MRS. WILLIAM BROWN MELONEY,
Secretary to the Advisory Council
for the "Better Homes" Campaign,
223 Spring Street,
New York City.

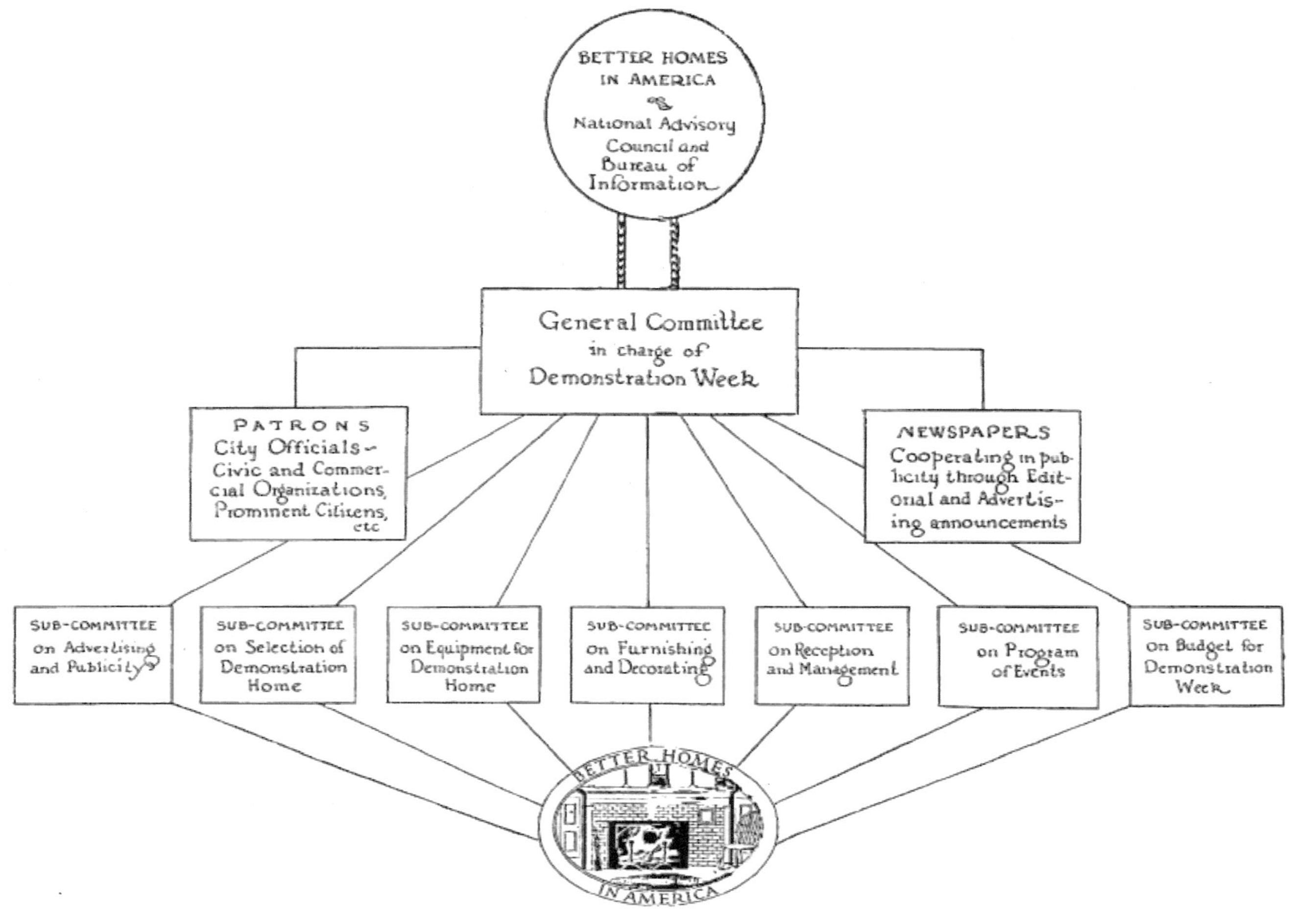

DEMONSTRATION OF BETTER. HOMES—October 9 to 14, 1922

A PLAN FOR COMMUNITY ORGANIZATION OF BETTER HOMES IN AMERICA

DEMONSTRATION WEEK OCTOBER 9TH TO 14TH, 1922

The future history of America will be shaped in large measure by the character of its homes. If we continue to be a home-loving people we shall have the strength that comes only from a virile family life. This means that our homes must be attractive, comfortable, convenient, wholesome. They must keep pace with the progress made outside the home. Realization of this has crystallized into a national civic campaign for Better Homes in America endorsed and encouraged by Federal and State officials and by prominent men in public life as set forth in this Plan Book.

The following plan has been prepared to give practical help to citizens of any community organizing for a *Better Homes in America* Demonstration Week, October 9th to 14th, 1922.

The Campaign in each community centers about a *Better Home*—completely equipped, furnished and decorated, in accordance with approved modern practice, and placed on exhibition during Demonstration Week.

Better Homes exhibitions have already been held, but now for the first time a national organization, endorsed and supported by the President of the United States and other Federal and State officials, is prepared to give practical help to every community wishing to share in the *Better Homes in America* movement.

The community which exhibits a *Better Home* during Demonstration Week will be given a powerful impetus for good. Every civic interest, every business and industry will be favorably affected. A *Better Homes* demonstration is a stimulus to better living, civic pride and community morale. It encourages thrift and industry. It develops a higher standard of taste. It means a better community in every way. This has been proved by the experience of many communities which have held successful exhibitions. They have ranged from cities as large as Cleveland, Milwaukee, Columbus, Kansas City and Dayton to villages of a few hundred population. In every case where the demonstration has been properly organized lasting benefits have followed.

FOLLOW THE PLAN

The National Advisory Council of *Better Homes in America*, through its Bureau of Information, has made a thorough investigation of previous exhibitions of this character.

This investigation has shown clearly that when the local organizations proceed in the right way a *Better Homes* demonstration may easily be made a great success. Causes of trouble as well as of success have been analyzed to bring out the methods that should be avoided. The Advisory Council, therefore, is in a position to recommend plans that have stood the test of practical experience.

With Federal and State governments endorsing and encouraging this Plan of educating the people to *Better Homes in America*, the conduct of local demonstrations is given tremendous impetus and support. And with the suggestions and the Plan for conducting such demonstrations herewith presented, any community may confidently undertake the production of a *Better Homes* Exhibition during Demonstration Week, October 9th to 14th, 1922.

A comparatively few energetic and capable women, with the support of local civic organizations, can effectively put into practice the ideas and plans with which they will be supplied by the Bureau of Information. The expense of a *Better Home* demonstration need not be great; in some communities it may be kept as low as $25.00. Builders, merchants and prominent citizens will combine to supply the Model *Better Home*, and to furnish it. Civic organizations and newspapers will cooperate to interest the public.

The most successful demonstrations have been so managed as to impress upon visitors that they were not selfish enterprises, intended to help special interests, particular firms or individuals. They have been so conducted as to benefit every line of business and to help the community as a whole. Neither the name of the builder or owner of the home exhibited, nor the name of any person or business firm furnishing any portion of the exhibit, is permitted to be displayed.

The motive behind the demonstration is primarily educational.

HOW TO FORM A GENERAL COMMITTEE
FOR BETTER HOMES DEMONSTRATION WEEK

A Better Homes Demonstration should be organized and directed by a disinterested group of prominent women, working from motives of public service. This group should be formed of a Chairman and a General Committee of from four to seven members, depending upon the size of the community.

Each member of the General Committee is Chairman of one or more sub-committees as outlined later in this Plan.

The Chairman of the General Committee is appointed through the National Advisory Council of *Better Homes in America*. She appoints the members of the local General Committee. They in turn appoint the members of the Sub-committees. In the case of the Sub-committees it is particularly important that appointments should be made with the knowledge and approval of the local civic and commercial interests whose co-operation is desired. Detailed suggestions for procedure are outlined later.

The duties of the members of the General Committee fit naturally into the following arrangement of Sub-committees with a member of the General Committee as Chairman of each Sub-committee:

(1) Sub-committee on Advertising and Publicity.

(2) Sub-committee on Selection of Demonstration Home.

(3) Sub-committee on Equipment of Demonstration Home.

(4) Sub-committee on Furnishing and Decorating.

(5) Sub-committee on Reception of Visitors and Management of Home.

(6) Sub-committee on Program of Events.

(7) Sub-committee on Budget for Demonstration Week.

Where the size of the community makes it desirable to have a General Committee of only four members, some such distribution of the Sub-committees as this is recommended:

(1) Chairman (a member of the General Committee) heading

    (a) Sub-committee on Advertising and Publicity; and

    (b) Sub-committee on Progress of Events.

(2) Chairman (a member of the General Committee) heading

    (a) Sub-committee on Equipment of Demonstration Home; and

    (b) Sub-committee on Furnishing and Decorating.

(3) Chairman (a member of the General Committee) heading

    (a) Sub-committee on Selection of Demonstration Home; and

    (b) Sub-committee on Reception of Visitors and Management of Home.

(4) Chairman (a member of the General Committee) heading

    (a) Sub-committee on Budget for Demonstration Week.

HOW TO SECURE PATRONS FOR BETTER HOMES DEMONSTRATION; FULL COOPERATION OF ALL LOCAL INTERESTS ESSENTIAL

Following the organization of the General Committee, the first duty of its Chairman should be the arrangement for meetings of the Committee—or its individual members—with the various City Officials, and Civic and Commercial Organizations in the community, to explain the Plan for a *Better Homes* Demonstration and to secure their endorsement and active support.

Those endorsing and supporting the Demonstration may be known as Patrons and should comprise the following:

    The Mayor
    Commissioner of Education (or Superintendent of Public School)
    Publishers or Owners of Local Newspapers

> Presidents of Important Women's Clubs
> President of Chamber of Commerce
> Agricultural Home Bureau, etc.
> President of Real Estate Board
> President of Rotary Club
> President of Kiwanis Club
> Presidents of Building & Loan Associations
> Presidents of other Business or Trade Associations related to the Home
>   Building and Furnishing Industries.

Churches should also be asked to support the movement.

Additional Patrons may properly be selected from prominent citizens of the community, who are noted for their public spirit and are not included in the above list.

The two essentials for a successful *Better Homes in America* Demonstration are genuine co-operation from all local civic, financial, commercial and educational interests, and full and extensive publicity through the local newspapers. From the youngest boy or girl scout to bank president, business man, school teacher, minister, manufacturer and city official, everybody in a community should have a real personal interest in the Demonstration. When the benefits of a successful *Better Homes* Demonstration are once understood this interest is readily aroused.

Investigation of successful exhibitions in Kansas City, Indianapolis, Cleveland and elsewhere proved conclusively that the cooperation of all local interests was the biggest single factor of success.

HOW TO FORM SUB-COMMITTEES

It is important to appoint as Chairman of each Sub-committee a member of the General Committee who is particularly fitted to the specific work assigned to her Sub-committee. The special abilities of the members of the General Committee should be taken into careful consideration and so used in the arrangement of the Sub-committees as to secure the best and quickest results.

The formation of Sub-committees is necessary not only to divide the work effectively, but also to arouse the interest and cooperation of the various local interests directly affected by home building and home betterment. All the local business groups—furniture dealers, hardware dealers, wall-paper and paint dealers, electrical dealers, real estate dealers, etc.—should be interviewed and asked to nominate a representative from each group to serve on the appropriate Sub-committee. In this way the appearance of favoring special interests will be avoided and the fullest co-operation secured.

It may be well to stress here that the Chairman of the General Committee should not become immersed in the details of the Sub-committees' work. She establishes a point of contact and a clearing house for *all* Sub-committees and directs the *Better Homes* Demonstration as a whole, but not in detail. Neither should the Chairman of a Sub-committee attempt to enter into details of the work of other

Sub-committees not under her direction. The Chairman of each Sub-committee is responsible to the Chairman of the General Committee, and to her alone.

Suggestions for the formation and activities of the various Sub-committees are given in the following:

I—HOW TO FORM SUB-COMMITTEE ON BUDGET FOR DEMONSTRATION WEEK

A member of the General Committee is the Chairman.

This Sub-committee should be made up of prominent citizens, representing both the financial and mercantile interests of the community. It would be appropriate to secure a Bank Cashier, who is accustomed to keeping accurate records of receipts and expenses, to act as Vice-chairman of the Sub-Committee. He may also act as Treasurer of the General Committee. This committee should have charge not only of the securing of the modest expense fund necessary for Demonstration Week, but also of the recording of facts and figures regarding the operation of the Demonstration Home, and the results obtained. Such a record will be exceedingly useful to the local General Committee as well as the National Advisory Council. Accurate figures on the local *Better Homes* Demonstrations will be invaluable in continuing the *Better Homes* in America Campaign, and arrangements have been made for prizes to be given to those Committees submitting the best reports and records of successful demonstrations.

SUGGESTIONS FOR THE SUB-COMMITTEE

There will be certain general expenses incurred in conducting a *Better Homes* Demonstration. These general expenses may range from $25 to $500 or more, depending upon the size of the committee and the extensiveness and completeness of the Demonstration.

Some of the items of expense which may be incurred are: insurance of borrowed property; special advertising in the form of street signs, window cards and posters; printing; prizes for contests; lecturers, and, possibly, special forms of entertainment.

In many communities where Demonstrations have been held, the small contributions necessary have been readily volunteered by the various organizations, business firms or individuals directly interested in the financing and furnishing of homes. Contributions may be secured from bankers, stores, public utilities, real estate dealers, building material dealers, insurance men, etc. The amounts contributed by the various interests should be carefully apportioned and only a sufficient sum collected to pay the actual expenses of the Demonstration.

In Dayton and other cities it was found that volunteer contributions were readily made by manufacturers of, or dealers in, trade-marked articles, such as pianos, vacuum cleaners, refrigerators, electrical equipment, etc. As these articles, because of the trade name affixed, received special advertising in the Demonstration Home, it was considered proper to accept contributions from the dealers. The selection of trade-marked articles which may be shown in a Demonstration Home should be made in a disinterested manner by the Subcommittee on Equipment.

2—HOW TO FORM SUB-COMMITTEE ON ADVERTISING AND PUBLICITY

A member of the General Committee is Chairman.

The success of the Demonstration rests largely upon the thoroughness with which this Committee does its work. It should, therefore, be composed of all of the Publishers or Advertising Managers of local Newspapers, and the Advertising Managers of Department Stores and other large business houses. The fullest co-operation should be secured from all the local publishing and advertising interests.

Local newspapers will gladly aid a *Better Homes* Demonstration, for such an exhibition presents unusual opportunities for selling advertising space to local merchants. In some of the cities where Demonstrations have been held, the newspapers have brought out large special editions carrying a great amount of local advertising, and filled with interesting and instructive reading matter regarding home building and home betterment.

SUGGESTIONS FOR THE SUB-COMMITTEE

The campaign publicity should commence with an announcement of the organization of the General Committee and the selection of Patrons. It should be continued, in advance of the opening of the Demonstration Home, by the use of reading matter descriptive of home planning, furnishing, decoration and equipment.

The local newspapers should co-operate with the Sub-committee in seeing that advertisements of exhibitors during the demonstration week do not mention the fact that the advertiser is an exhibitor. This, of course, should not preclude the general advertising of goods suitable for the equipment or furnishing of *Better Homes*. This regulation is in line with the non-commercial policy of the campaign, and merchants will readily understand its fairness.

This Sub-committee should provide painted signs announcing the location of the Exhibition Home. These signs should be placed at neighboring street intersections. Signs in the form of arrow pointers should be tacked on telephone poles in all parts of the city pointing in the direction of the Demonstration Home and announcing its exact location.

Automobile Posters or Banners for the cars of the members of the Committee may be furnished by local sign painters or printers.

The Committee should also see that show cards advertising the Demonstration are properly distributed and displayed in store windows and that posters are put up in suitable public places.

Show cards, posters and stickers bearing the imprint of the *Better Homes in America* campaign, with space left for local announcements, may be obtained by application to the Bureau of Information, *The Delineator*, 223 Spring Street, New York City, Secretary, Mrs. William Brown Meloney.

A circular descriptive of the show cards, posters and stickers may also be obtained through the Bureau of Information, which has arranged to have this advertising display matter prepared for the use of local Committees. It is strongly recommended that these posters and cards be used in order to standardize the various local Demonstrations.

The stickers should be widely distributed among local merchants for use on city mail during the week preceding and the week of the campaign.

Small electrotypes of the *Better Homes in America* campaign insignia, or trade-mark, may be obtained through the Bureau of Information for use on printed matter and in newspapers. They are shown in the circular descriptive of the advertising display material.

3—HOW TO FORM SUB-COMMITTEE ON SELECTION OF DEMONSTRATION HOME

A member of the General Committee is Chairman.

The selection of the home to be used for the Demonstration should be made by a *disinterested* committee. Experience has shown that this is the only satisfactory method, as all personal interests are thus eliminated and criticism avoided.

Previous experience also indicates that this Sub-committee, with a member of the General Committee as Chairman, of course, should be composed of the President of the local Real Estate Board (if there is one in the community), a representative of the Chamber of Commerce or Merchants Association, a representative architect, and a representative of the Building Material Dealers. Here again is illustrated the importance of securing the full co-operation of the various groups of business men directly affected by home building and owning. These groups should be interviewed and each group asked to appoint its representative on this committee. When the National campaign for *Better Homes in America*, and the Plan as outlined here, have been clearly explained to these interests, a Sub-committee for selecting the Demonstration Home may be organized, which will act disinterestedly and effectively.

SUGGESTIONS FOR THE SUB-COMMITTEE

The three cardinal principles to be observed in the selection of a Demonstration Home are: first, situation with respect to accessibility and nearness to street car lines; second, type of architecture; and third, cost.

A Demonstration Home should be situated within a reasonable distance of the business section of a community, and it should not be more than four blocks from the nearest street car line. In a city where the Demonstration Home was selected some eight blocks from the car line and upon a hill, the attendance was disappointingly small. The Demonstration Home should not be situated in the outskirts of a community. This was found to be a disadvantage in a city where a Demonstration Home was selected in a new, partially developed suburb, some distance from the city limits.

An extreme type of architecture should be avoided in a Demonstration Home.

With respect to the cost of the home selected, it has been shown in a number of cities that a house priced slightly above the average cost of homes in the community attracted the larger number of visitors. The public apparently likes to visit a home costing more than the average, because of a desire to see and admire better things. Demonstration Homes, therefore, may range in price from $5,000 to $15,000, including the land, but not including the furnishings and equipment.

Other essentials of an ideal home for demonstration purposes are fully outlined in an article prepared by direction of Secretary of Commerce Hoover and included in this Plan Book on pages 7 and 8. The builder or owner of the Home selected should be willing to loan it to the General Committee for the Demonstration Week, without charge. He should also be willing to landscape the grounds, decorate the walls and carry all insurance and damage risks. This has been gladly done by builders in Syracuse, Cleveland, Milwaukee, Kansas City and elsewhere. There is no better selling method for homes than that of putting on display a completely furnished and equipped home.

If the entire plan of campaign is explained to the builder or owner of a suitable home, and the advantages of indirect selling methods are pointed out to him, his co-operation will be readily secured.

The name of the builder or owner is not to be displayed on the Demonstration Home in any manner, shape or form, nor is his name to be carried in any of the advertising during the campaign.

This will do away with all appearance of favoritism in the choice of the house to be used. It is proper, however, to insert a reading notice in the newspapers announcing the selection of the Demonstration Home and giving the name of the owner or builder. No further reference should be made to him in any of the advertising matter during Demonstration Week, though the attendants in the home may properly give his name to any person inquiring for it.

4—HOW TO FORM SUB-COMMITTEE ON EQUIPMENT OF DEMONSTRATION HOME

A member of the General Committee is Chairman.

The selection and installation of all practicable labor-saving devices and appliances in the Demonstration Home is left to this Sub-committee. It should be composed of representatives of dealers in home equipment, architects, builders, and, if possible, a Home Demonstration agent of the Agricultural Department. (See announcement of special co-operation of Department of Agriculture by Secretary Wallace on page 9).

SUGGESTIONS FOR SUB-COMMITTEE

On pages 47-49 will be found a statement of the best modern practise in the equipment of a home permitting the most efficient and economical housekeeping.

It is probable that many communities will be unable to equip the Demonstration Home completely, in accordance with the standards laid down. So far as practicable these suggestions should be followed, but local conditions and the stock of equipment carried by local dealers may require some modifications in detail.

5—HOW TO FORM SUB-COMMITTEE ON FURNISHING AND DECORATING

A member of the General Committee is Chairman. In the selection of this Sub-committee the greatest care must be taken to secure the cooperation of all the business firms and individuals concerned in the furnishing and decorating of homes. Each group—furniture dealers, hardware dealers, paint and wallpaper dealers, department stores (if any), decorators (if any), art and book stores—should be interviewed on this important subject and asked to appoint representatives to serve on this Subcommittee.

SUGGESTIONS FOR SUB-COMMITTEE

In order to maintain the non-commercial aspect of Demonstration Week, no exhibitor's name should be displayed on any article shown in the Demonstration Home. No price tags should be permitted on any article. In this way all appearance of commercialism is avoided. This feature will appeal to the fair and broad-minded merchant and will secure the enthusiastic support of all the merchants in the community, no matter how small their business may be.

The attendants at the Home, in response to inquiries as to where certain articles may be secured, should be instructed to reply that they may be had from the inquirer's own dealer or from any dealer in the city.

In Dayton this non-commercial plan was wonderfully successful.

In communities where suitable furnishings and decorations are not obtainable from the local stores they may be borrowed from public spirited citizens, who have such articles as are adapted to the scheme of decoration and furnishing. For the guidance of the Sub-committee, which may not include expert decorators or furnishers as members, practical suggestions on good furnishing and decorating have been set forth on pages 30-42 of this Plan Book. These suggestions will undoubtedly prove helpful in assembling the furnishings and decorations for a Demonstration Home. If more detailed information is required, write to the Bureau of Information, *The Delineator*, 223 Spring Street, New York City, Secretary, Mrs. William Brown Meloney.

In all cases the basement of the Demonstration Home should be very carefully arranged, equipped and prepared for exhibition.

The furnishing of the Demonstration Home should include well-selected, standard home literature and reference books, properly arranged in book-cases or on shelves. A printed list of this selected library may be supplied for distribution to the visitors.

6—HOW TO FORM SUB-COMMITTEE ON MANAGEMENT AND RECEPTION

A member of the General Committee is Chairman.

The members of this Sub-committee should be selected for their ability to manage the Demonstration Home and to receive and care for the visitors. It may be composed of representatives of the various women's organizations in the city.

In order to insure the keeping of accurate records of attendance, one or more bank tellers should be members of the Sub-committee.

This Sub-committee is to provide the attendants at the Demonstration Home and to handle the visitors in such a way as to avoid confusion and damage. It should also keep an accurate record of attendance, of interesting inquiries and the general results. It should report in detail to the Budget Committee, so that the

General Committee may have an opportunity to compete for the prizes offered for the best report of a successful Demonstration.

SUGGESTIONS FOR THE SUB-COMMITTEE

During the hours of exhibition the Demonstration Home should be in charge of a capable woman of suitable personality. This may be a volunteer, or a paid worker, for the entire week, or several volunteer workers may undertake the management of the Home, having definite days of attendance assigned to them.

The hours of exhibition should be from 1:00 to 10:00 p.m. continuously. It has been found in exhibitions that the home need not be kept open during the morning hours. During this period it may be cleaned and placed in readiness for visitors.

An attendant for the bedrooms and two attendants for the first floor — one in the hall or living room and the other in the dining room and kitchen — will be required to direct and control the visitors and to keep the house in perfect order during the exhibition hours. These attendants may be club or committee members who volunteer their services for certain days in the week.

It has been noted in several exhibitions that visitors usually congregate at certain hours in the afternoon and evening, and frequently overcrowd upon the lawns. It is necessary, therefore, to erect light guard rails along the sidewalk leading from the street to the house. And it may sometimes be necessary to have an outside attendant who will keep the visitors in an orderly line of entrance. This is work that may very well be performed by Boy Scouts.

During times of congestion visitors should be taken through the house in groups not to exceed fifteen in number. They should be conducted through the rooms in an orderly manner by the attendants. In some cases it has been found advisable to send the visitors to the second floor first, so that they may depart through the kitchen after inspecting the first floor and basement. Girl Scouts may be used for conducting the visitors through the home.

A careful check on the attendance at the Demonstration Home should be kept. This can best be done by assigning a Boy or Girl Scout to count the visitors as they enter the home and keep an accurate tally, which should be reported to the manager in charge. In some cities it has been found that a list of visitors to the home may be readily obtained by having them register upon a numbered card, which can be used for a drawing contest — a prize being awarded to the lucky number. In smaller communities where the attendance will not be large at any one time the names of visitors may be kept in a small register or list book.

7—HOW TO FORM SUB-COMMITTEE ON PROGRAM OF EVENTS

A member of the General Committee is Chairman. This Sub-committee should be composed of persons who are particularly capable in arranging programs of entertainment, and may be selected from members of the Board of Education, School Principals and Teachers, Theatrical and Moving Picture Managers, Community and Song Leaders, etc.

THE FOLLOWING EVENTS ARE SUGGESTED

1—Sermons, Addresses and Sunday School talks in all churches on the Sunday preceding the opening of the exhibition.

2—Color slides relating to home owning, home management, home furnishing and decoration to be shown in moving picture houses.

3—Four-Minute Talks on thrift, home owning, home financing, home furnishing, home decoration, etc., in all moving picture houses.

4—Block Parties in front of the Demonstration Home. Lights for the block party may be supplied from the headlights and searchlights of automobiles properly arranged.

5—Window Dressing Contests for hardware merchants, house furnishing merchants, department stores, etc.

6—Erection of Miniature Home, suitable for a girl's playhouse, on Public Square—this playhouse may be given as first prize to the girl of school age writing the best essay on "Why You Should Own Your Home."

7—Showing special *Better Homes* films in all moving picture houses. (See special announcement on page 24.)

8—Prizes for the best example of a Model Kitchen in the community.

9—Cooking Demonstrations by Home Demonstration Agent, or some well-known local cook, High School or Normal School student.

10—Singing by Choir or Quartette on porch of Demonstration Home each evening at about 7:30 and 8:00 o'clock.

11—(a) Guessing contest as to how many visitors enter Demonstration Home.

11—(b) Prize for best essay by a boy on Home Owning.

(c) Prize for best essay by a girl on Home Equipment or Furnishing.

(d) Prize for best landscape design for Small Home by High School or Art student.

12—Radio Program at Demonstration Home, or elsewhere in the city.

13—Lectures on Home Equipment, Decoration or Furnishing by experts, in local auditorium. It has been found that admission to these lectures may be charged, to help defray the expense of lecturers.

LECTURE COURSES AND LECTURES

Lectures on Home Building, Furnishing, Decoration and allied subjects have been found to attract large audiences in cities where they have been given under the auspices of local organizations. Undoubtedly many communities co-operating in the *Better Homes in America* Demonstration Week, October 9th to 14th, will desire to include in their program of events lectures on *Better Homes* subjects.

BETTER HOMES IN AMERICA

Bureau of Information
The Delineator
223 Spring Street, New York City

Secretary, Mrs. WILLIAM BROWN MELONEY

The Bureau of Information has been established to support and coordinate the work of local *Better Homes in America* committees.

Additional copies of this Plan Book may be obtained from the Bureau of Information.

Other data and material will be supplied as indicated in the Plan Book.

Bulletins will be sent out from time to time to keep local committees posted on the national development of the *Better Homes in America* campaign.

In the following pages of the Plan Book are special articles prepared by governmental and other authorities on various phases of home building, equipment, decorating, sanitation, etc. The Bureau of Information will either answer inquiries in regard to any of these special articles or, when necessary, will refer the questions to the authors of the articles.

MOTION PICTURE PRODUCERS & DISTRIBUTORS OF AMERICA, INC.

522 FIFTH AVENUE
NEW YORK CITY

WILL H. HAYS president
COURTLAND SMITH SECRETARY
Telephone Vandebilt 2110

July 19, 1922

Mrs. W. B. MELONEY,
233 Spring Street,
New York City.

MY DEAR MRS. MELONEY:

I am immensely interested in the Better Homes Campaign. This is something that the motion picture industry should be interested in and I am sure that they will want to be.

I would like to help you to have available for your Better Homes week, October 9-14, pictures that would show clearly just what the modern home should be.

I am glad that the Better Homes Council has had such an encouraging response from the governors of the various states and from the women of this country. Certainly it is a matter to which all of us should give our very best. It will have an enduring influence on the lives of our people and it is one of the most creditable movements that I know of.

I have a little home in Sullivan, Indiana, that we are most anxious to equip in just exactly the best way, and I am as much interested as any one could be in learning how this should be done, so I am looking forward to October 9-14 with much interest.

With best wishes always, I am,
Sincerely yours,

Will H. Hays

ESSENTIALS FOR DEMONSTRATION HOME SUGGESTIONS ON BUILDINGS AND GROUNDS

BY JOHN IHLDER

DIRECTOR, HOUSING CONDITIONS,
CHAMBER OF COMMERCE OF THE UNITED STATES

Different parts of the country have quite distinct types of one-family dwellings. The best, unquestionably, is the detached house with adequate yard space on all four sides; the house which gets sun and air no matter which way it faces or what the direction of the prevailing breeze; the house whose yard makes it possible for the family, and especially for the children, to live much in the open. But, though this is the best type, it may prove impracticable for people of moderate means in communities where past practice has resulted in crowding the land to such an extent that group or row houses have become the standard.

Whatever the type of house, however, there are certain fundamentals of an essentially good house. The exhibition house should, as far as possible, embody these fundamentals as given below.

OPEN SPACE BELONGING TO THE HOUSE

If the house is of the detached type (open on all four sides) it should have a lot wide enough to permit fifteen feet of yard space on each side. Then it is protected from any danger of side windows being darkened and air cut off by any building which is permissible in a one-family house residence district (see Zoning and What it Means to the Home). Where there are no zoning regulations to give protection, even fifteen feet of side yard will not prevent injury from a tall apartment house or commercial building.

Under no circumstances should the demonstration house, if of the detached type, have less than ten feet of side yard. If no detached house with ten feet or more (preferably fifteen feet or a little more) of side yard can be secured, then seek a house of another type.

Next in order of excellence is the semi-detached house (twin — two houses side by side with a party wall). The single side yard of this house should be fifteen feet wide and never less than ten feet.

Next in order is the group house, or the row house. The row house may be a perfectly good house if it is wide enough in proportion to its depth so that there may be adequate open spaces before every window, and if it is so planned as to take full advantage of these open spaces. Moreover a row of houses may be so designed—perhaps as one unit so far as the front elevation is concerned—that they will be very attractive in appearance. A wide, row house (18 to 20 feet or more), properly planned, is much better to live in than a detached or a semi-detached house whose side yards are so narrow that they do not give adequate light and air to middle rooms.

The really good house is bright and airy. Consequently the demonstration house should be set back from the street and its front yard should be deep enough not only to assure privacy from the street, but also to permit at least a well sodded grass plot.

The rear yard will, of course, extend across the whole lot. Or the rear yard may be 100 feet deep. But in this connection, it is necessary to bear in mind that a yard may be too large as well as too small. It must fit in with the house, and some account must be taken of the probable habits of its occupants. A family which has no servants, and in which the breadwinner works long hours away from home, may find a large yard a burden unless some member is an enthusiastic gardener. Lacking this gardener the back of a deep yard is likely to become a dump-heap.

THE HOUSE ITSELF

Given adequate open space as described above there are certain essentials in the house itself.

CONSTRUCTION

A house is, or should be, an investment. Therefore it should be honestly constructed. One of the most important lessons for the home buyer to learn is that the initial cost of a house is not its full cost. It pays well to spend a little more on purchase price if, thereby, repair bills and maintenance costs are kept down. And it pays not only in dollars and cents but in satisfaction as well, for the house that soon begins to go to pieces, that soon looks shabby, is quite the opposite of a "joy forever."

Consequently the demonstration house should be well built, and one of the most valuable parts of the demonstration should lie in pointing out by suitable placards its structural excellencies. Has the ground immediately outside the walls been drained so that water will not lie against these walls and gradually soak into them? Is the cellar well drained and dry; well lighted and ventilated? Is the foundation well built? Are the beams and joists heavy enough and of good material? Are the floors and woodwork of good material, well seasoned, and of good workmanship? Is the hardware (locks, hinges, lighting fixtures, etc.) strong enough to stand usage? Are the outside walls of good material—if of brick, of good quality with good quality mortar; if of frame, of good lumber, well seasoned and well painted with three coats of paint? What kind of sheathing is used? Is wood well seasoned? Is the roofing of a material adapted to the climate and of good quality?

What material is used for flashing?

Recently there has been some discussion of the heat-retaining quality of walls. It is advocated that openings which permit circulation of cold air between outer and inner walls shall be filled. This adds but little to the cost of building and in cold climates reduces materially the coal bill. Incidentally it also aids both in reducing the fire hazard and in rat proofing. For the latter, care must be taken that there are no unscreened openings through foundation walls into a cellar, and that all openings from the cellar to the space between outer and inner walls of stories above shall be filled with rat-proof material.

Much attention is now being given to standardizing the parts of a house, both to reduce initial cost and to make replacement easier and less expensive. Are the doors, windows and other parts of the demonstration house of standard stock sizes?

LIGHT AND VENTILATION

Every room must have adequate window areas giving upon wide outdoor spaces. An interior room, or one poorly lighted from a narrow court, or receiving its only light from a wide porch, may not impress the visitor, who sees it only when the house is new and the room artificially lighted, but it does in time impress the family who inhabit it. Row houses are best when they are only two rooms deep from front to rear. If, however, an extension is built upon the rear of a row house, the court on one side of this extension, from which middle rooms are lighted, should be *at least six* feet wide for a two-story dwelling and seven feet for a three-story dwelling. If there is a front porch on a row house it should not extend clear across the front, darkening every window of the front ground-floor room, but should extend only part way, leaving one window free. This also adds to the value of the porch by giving it greater privacy, but of course it necessitates a house at least 18 feet wide, if the porch is to be large enough to use as an outdoor sitting room for the whole family in warm weather.

So far as practicable, each room should have at least two windows, and corner rooms should have windows in two walls.

The rooms should be planned so that they may be opened into each other and the breeze permitted to sweep through.

PRIVACY

While the family is a unit, and a function of the house is to symbolize and emphasize family unity, there should, nevertheless, be provision for some individual privacy. The most elementary provision, of course, is that there be at least three bedrooms—on the assumption that the normal family will contain both boys and girls. Consequently the demonstration house must contain not less than three bedrooms. But beyond this, the grouping of rooms possible in a two-story house (bedrooms and bath on the second floor, common living rooms on the first floor) as against a one-story house, adds greatly to privacy. At the same time the two-story house is nearly always the more economical both to build and to operate, while one flight of stairs does not add appreciably to the house-wife's work. With the kitchen, dining room, living room and a lavatory on the ground floor there is comparatively little need of running up and downstairs, even when there are young children in the family. A third story, an upstairs sitting room, no ground floor lavatory, do add appreciably to the amount of stair climbing.

Stair climbing is reduced by having the laundry on the same floor as the kitchen instead of in the basement or cellar. Though it is the scene of greatest activity only one or two days a week, it is often used at other times, and often in connection with kitchen work. On the score that the number of steps is thereby reduced, laundry tubs may be placed in the kitchen; but against this must be balanced the annoyance, or worse, that comes from having the kitchen full of steam and all cluttered up with clothes in process of washing when meals must be prepared. Because of this many women prefer a separate laundry in an ell or extension opening off the kitchen. From the latitude of Philadelphia south, this extension may be of light construction without danger of pipes freezing except in the coldest weather; and it is a simple matter to install a cut-off, so that these pipes may be emptied when not in use.

SANITATION

There should be a fully equipped bathroom on the bedroom floor and a toilet—preferably a wash bowl also—on the ground floor. A toilet in the cellar is only a half-way measure. It does give an added convenience of very real value, especially when there are servants; but it is usually less accessible than the upstairs bathroom and, unless the cellar is unusually well lighted and ventilated—unless it is heated and unless its floor is high enough above the sewer to provide for the necessary slope of the soil pipe—it is very likely to become a nuisance. A sewer-connected toilet in the yard is only a step above the old-time privy vault. It is inaccessible in bad weather; after dark it is public; and it is likely to freeze.

SUGGESTION FOR FURNISHING
AND DECORATING
THE DEMONSTRATION HOME
PREPARED BY THE BUREAU OF INFORMATION

Changing an empty house into a furnished, restful place of beauty is no less a task than transforming a piece of paper into a lovely picture. In one sense, interior decoration is a creative art. It is true that decorators, or persons furnishing houses, do not weave their own hangings, build their own furniture, or design their own wall-paper, but they select the things they require from shops, where they have been designed by others, and choose in such a way as to make a beautiful and harmonious whole.

Persons who must furnish a house for the occupancy of a family face four distinct problems: first, they must see that the things selected suit the house in size, coloring, and style; second, that the pieces selected are harmonious with each other, and that they are comfortable and well-made; third, that they suit the requirements of the family; and fourth, that they fit the family purse.

BACKGROUNDS

The first requisite of a house is that it be restful; therefore, it is wise to use wall coverings that are plain in effect. Plain paints or tints, and wall-papers of a cloudy, all-over pattern, make the best backgrounds.

When a room faces north, the best colors to use are the yellows, which might range from a cream color to a deep pumpkin yellow.

In rooms that face south, it is possible to use light grays, which might range to a deep putty color; though it is possible in sunny rooms to use almost any color except those which might fade easily.

The best way to treat rooms which have wide doorways connecting them with other rooms is to have the walls of both rooms alike, preferably in some plain color.

FLOOR COVERINGS

Rugs and floor coverings should be several shades darker than the walls, and be either in plain colors or have a small or indefinite all-over design. Where walls are plain, the latter type of carpet should be used. When walls have on them any figured covering, plain carpet should be used.

HANGINGS

The hangings for rooms which have plain wall coverings could be striped or figured, but in rooms where there is a figured wall covering, the hangings should be in plain colors, taking the color scheme for these from the dominating color note in walls and carpet.

FURNISHINGS

A good rule to follow in choosing furnishings is to avoid anything which strikes you as elaborate, or prominent. If a piece of furniture, carpet, or curtain material stands out in a shop, you may be quite certain that it will be even more noticeable in a house.

A house can only be considered properly furnished when it meets the real needs of the occupants. Comfortable chairs, sofas, and beds, good tables, and soft carpets, make up the most important objects, and these should be the best that the family can afford. No definite rule can be applied to the arrangement of the furniture, but balance and wall space should be considered first. Where a single opening is placed in the center of the wall, or like openings at equal distances, the wall spaces will be in balance; in the case of unequal openings, the wall spaces will be out of balance.

At balanced wall spaces, place pieces of furniture of relative size and contour. These may be tables, chairs, sofas, and pictures. Leave the more intimate and personal furniture, such as favorite chairs, sewing table, and foot stool, for a grouping at one side or in the center of the room. Lay all carpets and rugs parallel with the longest sides of the room.

In a room with unbalanced wall spaces, place against the longest spaces the largest pieces of furniture—the piano, the bookcase, the davenport—grouping perhaps a table, mirror, and chair against a smaller and opposite wall space. This permits the comfortable chairs, tables, lamps, and pottery to relieve the stiffness, allowing them to be grouped in the center of the room.

Do not indulge in too many pictures, but select a few of interest and good quality. These few should be hung on a level with the average eye. Small pictures should be hung somewhat lower.

Do not invest in many ornaments. A few bits of colored pottery, or some brass ware, is all that is required to strike a lively note. Place these so that they will balance other objects arranged on the same mantel or bookshelf. For example, a pair of brass candlesticks placed at either end of a mantel, with a pottery bowl, clock, or ornament in the center, strikes a balance. Never have a large jar on a small table or stand, or small ornaments on a large table. A good thing to remember is that ornaments decrease in value as they increase in number.

In the following pages will be found suggestive lists of articles which the rooms in a Better Home might contain. For further assistance and more detail, write the Bureau of Information.

SUGGESTIONS FOR FURNISHING THE HALL

HALL

A Modern Colonial Hall of good proportions and design, with the simple
but necessary furnishings for convenience and welcome.

The first impression of a house and its occupants comes as one enters through the front door into the hall. Thus, nowhere in the entire house is it more important to strike the right keynote in furnishing and decoration. If there is no closet in the hall for wraps and umbrellas, it will be necessary to have in some obscure corner a wooden strip painted the same color as the woodwork, in which are solid brass hooks, placed low enough so that the young members of the family can reach them. Also, for umbrellas, provide a plain pottery jar which will harmonize with the color scheme of walls and carpets.

On the hall table have a card tray—brass if the hardware is brass—silver if the hardware is nickel or iron—and a medium-sized pottery vase in crackle ware, or some natural color. A hall lantern or scones would be in harmony with these furnishings, and have decorative value.

A SUGGESTED COLOR SCHEME FOR THE HALL

Walls—Ivory paper or paint.

Woodwork—Paint—dull finish.

Floors—Hardwood—Stained antique oak, finished with wax or varnish.

Floors—Softwood—Painted a deep yellow, or gray, or stained to represent hardwood.

Floors—Linoleum—In a tile pattern of black and white, provided the living room is not directly connected with the hall; in such case use only plain brown, grey, or Jaspe linoleum.

BELOW IS A SUGGESTED LIST OF FURNISHINGS WHICH THE HALL MIGHT CONTAIN

A table—Of oak, mahogany, or walnut, either drop-leaf, gate-leg, or console.

A mirror—Gilt, or to match the wood in the table, Early American or English.

A straight chair or two—With or without rush seats, enameled black, with stencil design, or to match the wood of the tables.

A low-boy—Of mahogany or walnut, with drawers for gloves, string, etc.

A large chest—Of oak or brass-trimmed mahogany, for overshoes, etc.

One or two rugs—May be *Oriental* in blues, browns, tans or black; or wool braided, in blues, browns, tans or black; or Wilton, in blues, browns, tans or black; or Axminster, in blues, browns, tans or black.

A cocoa mat placed at front door.

THE LIVING ROOM

As the living room is the gathering place for family and friends, it may well be considered the most important room in the house. It should take its keynote for decoration from the hall. If there is a wide doorway connecting the living room with the hall, the color scheme should be the same. As the living room serves as library also, open book shelves, painted the same as the woodwork, are essential, and more substantial than book cases.

The first requisite of such a room is that it shall be restful. Avoid using rocking chairs. Use little bric-a-brac. Nothing which does not contribute to the necessity and beauty of the room should be allowed.

Tan or ivory is good in a room which is inclined to be dark, or gray and gray-green in a room inclined to be bright.

A SUGGESTED COLOR SCHEME FOR LIVING ROOM

Walls—Ivory, cream or gray—paper or paint.

Woodwork—Ivory paint—dull finish.

Floors—Hardwood—Stained antique oak with wax or varnish finish.

Floors—Softwood—Painted a deep yellow or gray, or stained to represent hardwoods.

A SUGGESTED LIST OF FURNISHINGS FOR LIVING ROOM

Table—Drop-leaf—in mahogany, weathered oak, or walnut; Gateleg—in mahogany, weathered oak, or walnut; Modern Chippendale—mahogany, weathered oak, or walnut, or Sheraton type of table.

Sofa—Upholstered in either sage green or brown upholsterer's velvet; blue, yellow, mauve satin or taffeta sofa cushions.

Armchair—Overstuffed chair in indefinite striped upholsterer's velvet in sage green; satin cushion in corn color.

Armchair—Back and seat upholstered in brown like sofa—arms of mahogany.

Desk—A reproduction of a Sheraton, Hepplewhite, or Early English Desk.

Chair—Rush bottom—same wood as desk, or in dull black or sage green dull enamel, conventional stencil design.

Wicker chair—Of brown or natural wicker, with printed linen cushions in floral pattern.

Tilt table for cards or tea—Mahogany or walnut.

Fireplace (If any)—A wood-box or basket; andirons and fire screen, hearth brush and tongs.

A Reading Lamp—Sage green or black pottery base; an old gold colored paper shade, fluted or plain, top and bottom bound with sage green tape ribbon, or guimpe.

A Clock—In simple, plain design of wood, antique gilt, or leather.

Footstool—Small ottoman, covered in black and yellow needlework, or velvet same as sofa (brown).

Waste paper basket—Small black wicker next to desk.

Decorative Accessories—Green vase, gold luster bowl, mauve pottery piece; Desk appointments in dull brass, bronze, or leather; Book-ends—Library Shears. Match box and ash tray on table in brass or bronze.

Carpet—One large or several small Orientals, or a Wilton, Axminster, or velvet in two tone of brown or tan, or in plain colors. *Glass curtains*—Cream, marquisette, cheese-cloth, or scrim, made plain.

Overdraperies—(If desired)—Can be either printed linen, same as cushion in wicker chair, lined with sage green sateen, or brown or sage green poplin, silk damask or sunfast.

Chairs—If the room is large enough, one or two chairs, chosen to correspond with those already in the room, may be added.

DINING ROOM

The dining room should be one of the most cheerful and inspiring rooms of the house. It is the place where the family gathers to enjoy meals together, and nothing insures a better start than having breakfast in a bright, cheerful room.

If the dining room and living room are connected by wide doorways, have the walls of both rooms alike. If they are connected by a small door, the walls may be in some light cloudy landscape paper, or in a small allover pattern in light cream, buff, gray, tan, or putty color. Because there is so much blue china, persons feel that they want blue dining rooms. This is a mistake, as blue used in large quantities in either walls, china, or hanging absorbs the light and makes a room gloomy. Do not display china or glassware in a so-called china closet. A built-in corner cupboard, or a small mahogany or rosewood cabinet, which might hold rare bits of pottery and china, is permissible. It is far better to use the pantry shelves for china than to crowd it into a china closet.

It is best to use a rug with small figures. The hangings should be in plain colors, taken from the predominating colors in the wall covering; or if the walls are the same as the living room, the hangings should be chosen from the predominating color in the living room. This will bring the rooms into perfect harmony, without having them just alike.

SUGGESTED COLOR SCHEME FOR DINING ROOM

Walls—Ivory or cream, if closely connected with living room. A cloudy landscape, crepe, or cartridge paper in buffs, pale grays, fawn, or cream if closed off from living room.

Woodwork—Ivory.

Floors—Hardwood—Stained antique oak, with wax or varnish finish.

Floors—Softwood—Painted a deep yellow or gray, or covered in plain brown, gray, or Jaspe linoleum.

DINING ROOM

This well-proportioned dining room with its plain walls and figured
floor covering has a square mahogany table and eight chairs of the
Georgian period.

SUGGESTED LIST OF FURNITURE FOR DINING ROOM

Table—Round or square extension, or drop-leaf—six legs—in mahogany, walnut, weathered oak, or painted black, gray, or coco. Might be reproduction of Hepplewhite, Sheraton, or Georgian period. A glass, silver, or pottery bowl, containing flowers, on the table; plain ecru linen doilies.

Chairs—8 chairs—Mahogany—Damask seats, Hepplewhite backs. Walnut—English linen seats, Sheraton backs. Weathered Oak—Velvet Seats, Queen Anne backs. Painted—Rush seats, or wooden seats, Windsor or straight backs.

Sideboard—Low, broad, after Hepplewhite or Sheraton, a Welsh dresser with Windsor chairs. (Here keep either a few good pieces of silver with candlesticks on either end, or a large pottery bowl filled with fruit in the center, and candlesticks to match the bowl placed at either end, or some bits of red or yellow glass, but do not combine all three. Do not use delicate lace runners or doilies. Plain linen, or heavy real filet is far more effective Display no cut glass or hand-painted china.)

Mirror or Mellow, dark-toned painting—Framed in antique gilt or to correspond with the wood of the furniture selected, and hung on level with the eye, directly in the center and over the sideboard.

Serving Table—To correspond with other furniture selected, and placed as near the kitchen door as possible.

Here keep two or four silver or glass candlesticks which are used on the table at night, also a silver, mahogany, or wicker tray.

Mirror—Queen Anne type—over serving table—especially if serving table is between two windows, it gives effect of space.

Muffin stand—Especially for maidless house—of mahogany, walnut, or painted to correspond with furniture selected.

Nest of Tables—Small, square, of either mahogany, walnut, or black lacquer, to be kept in a corner and used for tea parties, functions, etc.

Rug—Large Oriental—In blues, yellows, browns, or old rose and black; Wilton—in blues, yellows, brown, or old rose, and black; Axminster—in blues, yellows, browns, or old rose, and black; Chenille or velvet, in plain colors.

Curtains—Glass curtains to match living room, in either marquisette, cheese cloth, or scrim, made plain.

Overdraperies—If desired, can be either like the living room, if rooms are in close proximity, or taken from the predominating color note of living room hangings if these are figured.

With a cloudy or landscape paper, use plain poplin, rep, or sunfast, in warm tans, sage green, with bands of black or orange, or both, across the bottom; this would give character to the room.

Uniformity in furniture chosen—Be sure in choosing your furniture that uniformity is observed as to period, wood, and type. For example, if a Sheraton sideboard in mahogany is selected, then the entire furniture of the dining room should be of the Sheraton type in mahogany.

BEDROOMS

The first requisite in furnishing a bedroom is that it appears crisp and clean. The walls, light in color, must be restful and simple in design. The woodwork should be white, if possible. Painted furniture is very popular for a bedroom because of its dainty appearance, but dull-finished mahogany or walnut in four post or Colonial design, with rag, braided, or hooked rugs, makes a charming bedroom.

Place the bed where the sleeper will not be subject to strong light or cross drafts (see page 27 for proper ventilation). A dressing table is fashionable, but not as practical as a chest of drawers with mirror above. A full-length mirror installed in a closet door, or hung in a narrow wall space, is a very decided adjunct. Be sure to place the dressing table or chest of drawers where the light is not reflected from an opposite window. To secure a good view, the light should be directed upon the person to be reflected, and not upon the mirror.

Avoid placing the furniture all on one side of the room. If possible, intermingle high and low pieces to secure a proper balance. If one bed is used, be sure to place beside it a table on which should be a lamp, telephone, and small water bottle and glass. If two beds are used, place this table between the two beds.

If the walls are plain in color, figured draperies and bedspreads can be used. If the walls have on them a small design, plain materials fur these purposes should be used.

SUGGESTED COLOR SCHEME FOR BEDROOM

Walls—Corn colored cross-bar paper.

Woodwork—White, dull finish, paint.

Floors—Hardwood—Stained antique oak, with wax or varnish finish.

Floors—Softwood—Painted a deep yellow, or covered in plain brown, tan, or Jaspe linoleum.

Suggested List of Furnishings for the Bedroom

Bed—Full size, or twin beds—In mahogany, walnut, ivory paint, or enamel. Box or wire springs. Mattress and pillows.

Bedspreads and bureau covers may be made of unbleached muslin, bound with wide bands of plain yellow, blue, and brown, these colors overlapping each other, or plain white Swiss, dimity, or Marseilles.

One high-boy, or high chest of drawers for man—In mahogany, walnut, or painted. This piece should conform with or match other furniture in room. Brushes, comb, box for odds and ends, clothes brush.

Mirror—Hung flat against the wall—in same wood as high-boy.

One Dressing Table—or low chest of drawers—for lady—with mirror hung over the chest of drawers. May be in mahogany, walnut, or painted. With toilet articles in silver or tortoise shell, or ivory; pin cushion, scent bottles. The mirror may be of Queen Anne type in antique gilt, to correspond with woods used in room.

Two straight back chairs—In mahogany, walnut, or painted, with plain wood, rush, or caned seats.

Natural wicker arm chair—Sturdy type placed near window, with cushions of chintz or sateen to match the bedspreads.

Small flat-top desk and chair—In either mahogany, walnut, or painted, to correspond with furniture.

Supply with note paper, silver or brass ink-well, and blue feather pen.

Small Sewing Table—Of Martha Washington design, or a Colonial type, in mahogany or rosewood. Place on it small lamp with base of wood, in brown or tan porcelain, and having a shade of blue silk lined with tan silk.

A Chest—In either cedar, mahogany, or cretonne-covered, and placed under a window or in a corner for storage of summer or winter clothes.

Rugs—Oriental in black, blues, or yellows, plain brown or tan carpet, made into a large rug, or wool braided, hooked, or heavy rag rugs, in black, blues, tans, browns.

Small rugs should be placed near the bed, dressing table, and high-boy.

Curtains—Glass curtains of scrim, marquisette, or cheese-cloth, to correspond with those of living room and dining room.

Draperies—Draperies of either cretonne or muslin to match bedspreads, with bands of yellow, blue and brown sateen to correspond with bedspreads.

BEDROOM FOR EITHER BOYS OR GIRLS

It has been proven that furnishings and color produce either desirable or disastrous effects upon the sensitive minds of children. As all children's rooms are usually a combination of bedroom, play room, and study, it is well to keep in mind colors, design, arrangement, and practicality for all purposes.

To most children, a spotty or too often repeated design is distracting. Blues and violets soothe, while reds, yellows, and sometimes greens are exciting and stimulating colors. We so often send our children to study and amuse themselves in their room, but have we done our share in providing them with the comforts and necessities that will assist them to produce better school work?

Boys—With no frills, light fabrics, or woodwork for them to soil and mar, their rooms still may be made interesting—even beautiful—but convenience and masculinity should be kept foremost in mind.

Girls—A girl's room, on the other hand, should be dainty, bright, and frivolous. Her personality, even at a very tender age, will clearly be disclosed by the way she cares for her room. There is no need of a great expenditure of money in buying furniture or hangings for a girl's room. Some of the cheaper fabrics and simplest furniture will make the most charming room.

BOY'S ROOMS

A Suggested Color Scheme

Walls—Buff-colored paint, or tinted walls.

Woodwork—Stained mission oak or walnut.

Floors—Hardwood floor, strips of coco matting, or woolbraided rugs. Softwood—a large square of linoleum.

SUGGESTED LIST OF FURNISHINGS

Bed—Something of the day bed type. Bedspread of blue denim, with stitched bands of yellow sateen at edge.

Chest of Drawers—Painted buff or brown, or walnut or mission oak.

A Mirror—Antique gilt, or of wood to match chest of drawers, hung low.

A Desk—Of the craftsman type, with stool or bench to match.

Two Wooden Chairs—Either painted or of mission oak.

A Table—Low, plain wooden table, of walnut, or stained to match the woodwork.

One Comfortable Chair—Brown wicker, or the Windsor type.

A Lamp—Of the student type, or on a bracket, securely fastened on the wall.

A Tie Rack—Hung near chest of drawers.

One or two shelves—For books, trophies, etc. Made of plain wood, stained to match the woodwork of a plain bookcase of mission oak.

Curtains—Of blue denim, with stitched bands of sateen at edge—hung straight.

GIRLS' ROOMS
A Suggested Color Scheme

Walls—Papered in a soft gray-rose, allover design paper.

Woodwork—Cream paint.

Floor—Hardwood—Rag rugs, with rose stripes or a gray chenille carpet. Softwood—Battleship gray paint, with rag rugs or rose chenille carpet.

SUGGESTED LIST OF FURNISHINGS

Bed—Single—Painted ivory or cream—four post, or with some low, simple headboard.

Bedspread of rose dotted swiss, with wide ruffle.

A Dressing Table—To match bed, with rose colored sateen mats—bound in pale-gray with drawers.

A Large Box—For waists, etc. Covered in rose and gray cretonne.

A Desk—To correspond with painted furniture; a gray blotter and rose colored pen.

Two Chairs—One of natural wicker with cushions of rose sateen, and one of wood to correspond with painted furniture, caned seat.

A Sewing Table—Of mahogany or cherry.

A Lamp—China base with a shade of silk, dotted swiss, or rose-colored paper.

THE NURSERY

The ideal nursery is also a play room. It should, as nearly as possible, meet the ideals of the child's own world. In that room are received early impressions which are never forgotten, and which have a lasting influence on the adult life.

Don't bedeck the cribs, beds, or curtains with ribbons and laces, and expect your child to be happy. The "don'ts" and "be carefuls" make children irritable and unhappy. Choose the room with a thought to sunlight, and be sure it has outside blinds which will darken the room without keeping out the air.

The floor should be bare with the exception of one rug near the bed, or should be covered with a good grade of plain linoleum.

The walls and woodwork should be painted, if possible, a cream or light gray. Some fairy tale friezes are attractive, and afford opportunities of introducing color, but, if used, should not be placed too high on the wall—about three-quarters of the way up from the floor is a reasonable height. Child-study has taught that many and oft-repeated designs and subjects become meaningless, especially to older children.

The furniture in the nursery should be practical. Painted furniture and wicker chairs are attractive. A comfortable winged or overstuffed chair for the grown-ups is essential. Low shelves and cupboards, built for toys and books, are necessary if the room is to be kept neat and tidy. A stationary blackboard, and a large box for books and cherished belongings, are very welcome additions.

A SUGGESTED COLOR SCHEME FOR THE NURSERY

Walls—A soft, misty, gray paint, tint, or plain paper.

Woodwork—A dull white.

Floors—Plain hardwood, with a rag or braided rug in sapphire blue—or softwood, entirely covered in taupe Jaspe linoleum.

BELOW IS A SUGGESTED LIST OF FURNISHINGS WHICH THE NURSERY MIGHT CONTAIN

A Crib—White iron or wood, on ball bearing casters.

Bedspread of yellow and white seersucker, or a silky yellow sunfast.

A Tall Chest of Drawers—Painted cream or white, with plenty of drawers.

Table—Low nursery table or tall one which has had its legs cut.

Two Chairs—Low, with wooden seats, and painted to match the furniture.

A Desk—Flat top with plenty of paper and pencils.

Waste Paper Basket—White or natural wicker.

One Large Fireside Chair—With slip cover of blue and yellow striped linen.

Glass Curtains—Of best quality of cream colored cheesecloth, bound in yellow tape.

Over draperies (If desired)—Of primrose yellow silk, or sunfast, or striped yellow and blue linen to match slip cover.

Clothes Rack—Low wooden rack, painted white, with at least four hooks.

Closet—Should have a low pole on which could be hung plenty of hangers. Also a shelf about 6 inches from the floor for shoes, etc.

Large Cushions for the floor—One each of blue, yellow, nile green and orange.

Color Scheme—If you desire another color scheme, such as blue-and-white, or pink-and-white, write for information.

MODEL KITCHEN

PREPARED BY THE HOME ECONOMICS BUREAU
OF THE DEPARTMENT OF AGRICULTURE

The first consideration in arranging kitchen equipment is to save steps and labor. The kitchen should be clean, odorless and attractive.

Size — Not more than 120 square feet of working space for preparing food and washing dishes. More space when kitchen is used for laundry or has dining alcove.

Ventilation — If no cross drafts are provided for, cut a transom over back door if possible and arrange window boards to allow ventilation through top and bottom of window. Is desirable to have hood installed over stove to carry off drafts.

Lighting — Two or three windows desirable and a glass pane in kitchen door. If unavailable, increase light by having very pale walls and mirrors in dark corners. Artificial light should be from powerful burner hung from center of ceiling. Electric light should be indirect. Additional side lights should be added near sink and stove, unless they receive full light.

Wall Coverings — (1) Commercial oil cloth wall covering; or (2) good oil enamel paint. Color — Light tones. On Southern exposure — pale gray, green or pale blue; on Northern exposure — buff walls with a deeper buff or tan woodwork are good. For very dark rooms — white. Avoid white in well lighted rooms because of glare. If natural color, woodwork should have two coats of water proof varnish; if painted, two coats of flat paint and one of enamel paint.

Floor Coverings — If room has cement floors, provide rubber mats before sink, stove and cabinet to avoid foot strain. Otherwise, use linoleum slightly darker than walls and harmonizing or contrasting in color; or any other surface easy to keep clean.

LIST OF KITCHEN FIXTURES

The Kitchen should have the following equipment:

Range — Coal, wood, gas, oil or electric. Good hood for ventilation is desirable. Height of all working surfaces depends upon height of woman who will work in kitchen. All working surfaces including top of range should be as near the same height as possible. Height should be at least 32 inches, or more, if worker is tall. A label should state this fact. If coal range is the main one, have supplementary gas, electric or oil range. Gas range should have stove pipe from oven.

Sink — Sink should be large enough to accommodate both a washing and rinsing dish pan. Have large drain board on each side with raised edge or beading.

It should either slope gradually toward sink or have sloping grooves. If only one drain board is provided, add an adjustable folding board. Bottom of sink should be at least 32 inches from floor. Sink should be placed under or near a window to insure coolness and view.

Cabinet—White or colored enameled metal or natural wood finish with broad working shelf 32 inches from floor or higher according to height of worker. Shelves and bins for most commonly used supplies and utensils. If a cabinet with a good work shelf is not available an additional table near cabinet should be provided.

Tables—One or two tables, porcelain, glass, enamel, or zinc topped. If none of these can be had, linoleum may be fitted with waterproof cement to a wooden table. It should be at least 32 inches high. A table with drawers underneath and a swinging stool and space for knees is good.

Cupboard—If there is no dining room pantry, a cupboard should be added for the china; if space permits, this should be added anyhow for less frequently used utensils and supplies.

Stool—Stool, preferably white, should be of right height to allow sitting at table, work-shelf or sink. Add a plain chair if space permits.

Refrigerator—A well insulated ice box, preferably white. Ice compartment should be at side or top. Straight easily cleaned drain pipe should attach to plumbing. If refrigerator is indoors a door for icing from the outside is desirable.

Towel Rods—Wood or nickel with space for four or five dish towels.

Hand Towel Rack—If only one person uses it, roller towel rack may be installed. Otherwise, paper toweling or individual hand towels hung on cup hooks near sink by loops on corners.

Wall Clock—Simple, with clear figures.

Housekeepers' Rest Corner—If space permits, a comfortable chair, footrest and small table for books and sewing should occupy a little-used portion of the room, to permit rest and recreation while waiting for food to cook.

Garbage Pail—Covered; with foot lever to raise cover without stooping; fireproof trash basket.

ARRANGEMENT OF EQUIPMENT

Sink, cabinet with broad working shelf and dish cabinet (if dishes are washed in kitchen) should be as close together as possible without cramping passage room. Stove should be convenient to, but slightly away from, work shelf for hot weather. An ideal arrangement is china cupboard at right of sink, cabinet with broad work shelf at left of sink and, in a narrow kitchen, range on opposite wall from sink across narrowest part of room; if range is far from any broad working surface a table should be very near range. All kitchen equipment, except range, should be as near as possible to dining room door. If no dining room pantry with sink is provided, kitchen sink should be near dining room door. Range with supplementary range beside it should be so placed that full day light will light the oven. If stove is already installed in a dark place in exhibition house, move it into light, even though repiping and wiring may be required. Mirrors may be hung to throw additional light on range. If there is no good working shelf on cabinet, a table should be near cabinet for mixing food. There will then have to be a second table with a heat proof top near the stove unless stove is so near to cabinet that one table will serve both for mixing and setting hot utensils on. If possible, install a gas range, or an electric range if current is cheap enough to warrant. The range should, if possible, have an oven heat regulator. Where gas is unavailable and cost of electric current high, install a good oil stove with an oven. Refrigerator should be on porch or vestibule just outside kitchen door or should be in the kitchen near the back door away from the stove. If space permits, table next to refrigerator is a convenience. An out-icer is a convenience; in cold weather the ice compartment may be left empty and open for the air to cool the food.

Dish towel and hand towel racks should be as near as possible to sink, high enough to be out of the way. The dish towel rack should be on side towards window for drying and airing.

Wall clock should be within sight of stove without worker turning around. Garbage pail and trash basket should be under sink. Stove should be near chief working surface; either table or cabinet.

Decorations—Simple, easily washed curtains of gingham, striped calico or unbleached muslin with a colored tape border add to the attractiveness of the room. They should not obscure the light. If the windows are near working centers, curtains may be half length, that is, from top of window to center sash, and finished with a fringe.

Smaller up-to-date equipment, such as a fireless cooker, a pressure cooker, utensils, electric whippers, cutlery, strainers and so on, should also be installed. Further information is given in another bulletin.

THE KITCHEN AS LAUNDRY

If the Kitchen is also used as Laundry, laundry equipment should be away from cooking equipment if possible. *Two Tubs*—well-lighted, tops 34 inches, a *Washing Machine* run by whatever power the locality affords, preferably electricity. Washing Machine may have direct connection with plumbing, or good pipe hose should be provided for draining and filling machine. Copper lined *Wash Boiler* with spigot for emptying. *Zinc Topped Table*—on rollers, same height as top of stove, for carrying wash-boiler between sink and stove. *Ironing Board*—If possible, board that folds into cupboard. Board should have its own support far enough in from ends to permit of putting garment over it. *Clothes Basket—with Casters on Bottom.*

Iron—Electric Iron, or if electricity is unavailable, gas iron. Electric or hand *Mangle* for ironing.

Have tubs, washing machine, ironing board and plug for electric iron grouped together.

THE EQUIPMENT OF THE HOUSE

Having a house that is structurally sound, well planned and with adequate yard space, the next question is its equipment. Equipment has to do with the operation, with the house work. On the one hand this is more or less determined by the size and plan of the building, on the other by the furnishing and decoration. A well planned house makes house work lighter; and furnishing and decoration which add unnecessarily to the number of things which must be cleaned or cared for, or heavy pieces which must be moved, add to the labor of house work. Nevertheless, equipment occupies a clear outfield of its own that calls for separate discussion.

HEATING

Central Heating—Central heating preferred. May be hot air, steam, hot water, or vapor. Insulate heater and pipes. Large furnace water pan, or radiator water-pans, desirable. Select heating system, using fuel most economical for your locality. Thermostat heat regulator installed in living room is desirable. Write placards describing why you selected this heating plant; why it is so well insulated; why large water pan or radiator water pans are important.

Supplementary Heat—Open fireplace, Franklin stove or gas logs desirable in living room for beauty and comfort in spring and fall.

WATER SUPPLY

Should have running hot and cold water. If city water not available, should be pumped by power rams. Hot water boiler may be attached to coal range with auxiliary gas or oil heater for summer. Where gas rate is low, gas may be used alone. Automatic gas hot water heaters very desirable.

BATHROOM

Size—Should be large enough for tub, basin, toilet, clothes-hamper, stool, medicine cabinet and towel cabinet.

Floor—Should be most sanitary. Tile, stone or linoleums are the most sanitary. Small black and white pattern or light blue and white are good. A well-filled painted wood floor of battleship gray or colonial buff may be used.

Walls—Tile or plaster painted with two coats flat paint and one coat of enamel, or oil cloth wall covering. White, blue and cream are the best colors.

Ventilation—Window board should be in window to allow top and bottom ventilation. An additional separate ventilator is desirable.

Fixtures—Porcelain or enameled iron tub with hot and cold running water; shower with spray set at angle not to wet hair.

Basin—Porcelain or enamel with hot and cold water. *Toilet*—porcelain, white enameled seat desirable. *Medicine Cabinet* with door and mirror over basin, shelves for shaving equipment, lotions, antiseptics, etc. *Cupboard* large enough to hold supply of towels, soap, toilet paper, and equipment for cleaning bathroom fixtures.

Clothes hamper unless chute to bin near wash tubs is provided. Hamper should have white smooth surface. Enameled metal or wood desirable.

Towel racks—A nickel or enameled wood rack for each member of family to keep towels separate.

Miscellaneous fixtures—Two nickel or enameled metal soap racks, one beside basin and one beside or hooked to tub. Tooth brush rack to hold tooth brushes well separated. Toilet paper basket or rack. Individual mugs or glasses for each member of family. Shelf of glass or wood covered with oil cloth over basin.

Stool—White enamel, preferably. *Clothes hooks* on back of door, or clothes tree. *Sash curtains* of white material, easy to launder.

Lavatory—It is well to have additional lavatory on ground floor to save steps. It should contain toilet, wash bowl, stool and fixtures for accessories. Should be as easy to clean and hygienic as bathroom.

LIGHTING

Electricity if possible. Bulbs in all rooms should be frosted or shaded. *Hall*—Electricity or lamp hung from center in form of lantern or cast iron bracket to hold at least one bulb or one lamp. If side lights are desired, fixtures of brass, cast iron, or enameled iron are effective.

Living Room—If possible, at least one baseboard plug, one center ceiling light or side brackets if desired. If room is large a center floor plug is desirable. Plugs permit lamps to be used without unnecessary cords showing. If wire must pass through rug, do not cut rug but push threads apart.

Dining Room—If a center light in shape of dome is used, hang low enough to avoid shining in eyes of those dining. A soft effect is gained by side brackets representing sconces. Wired metal or glass candlesticks on mantel and side-board, give pleasing effect. Floor plug near dining table for electrical table appliances.

Bedrooms—Fixtures should be placed in long wall space convenient to bureau or dressing table. Have plug near bed for lamp for reading in bed. If space permits, night light on table in upper hall is useful. All plugs and sockets should be of standard shape and size.

CLEANING

House should be easy to clean with hard smooth floors, with cracks well filled, and rugs rather than carpets. Rounded edges and corners of baseboards desirable, also simple baseboards. One flight of stairs is sufficient if located out of sight of living room. This saves labor of cleaning two flights. Two cleaning closets, one on ground floor and one on second floor, are labor savers. Have space for vacuum cleaner and for hanging all brushes, brooms and dusters, and a shelf above or at side for the cleaning compounds. Zinc or other fireproof lining to cupboard and ventilator desirable.

Storage Space—Attic with rows of shelves for storing boxes and small objects is desirable. Wooden chests, trunks, and a cedar lined chest or cupboard useful. Built-in closets or rows of inexpensive chests of drawers with space to pass between are good.

STORAGE CLOSETS

Every bedroom should have clothes closet with hooks and a rod for hangers, a shelf for hats and a bottom shelf for shoes. A tall closet may have near ceiling an additional rod for hangers for less often used clothes, and long rod lifter to reach hangers. A cupboard for bed linen should be in upstairs hall or in a centrally located room. On ground floor coat closet is desirable; also tool cupboard or chest, large china cupboard, low enough for all china to be within reach. Cold closet with open wire screen cabinets in basement.

PANTRY

If kitchen is well ventilated and stove has hood, pass pantry not necessary. It makes extra steps. If pass pantry is in house, only its narrowest dimension should divide kitchen from dining room. Partitions under sink for trays to stand; a narrow space for table leaves; a china cupboard with reachable shelves, and a sink and drainboards like those described for kitchen are desirable. Drawer on small shelf for cleaning compounds and brushes for cleaning silver, steel, brass and copper.

FINANCING A HOME

PREPARED BY THE DIVISION OF BUILDING AND HOUSING, DEPARTMENT OF COMMERCE

1.—WHAT YOU BUY AND HOW TO BUY IT

In purchasing a home a misstep may be unfortunate, so get the best advice you can, and watch every step. First of all, what you buy is the site and the improvements on it. If a building and loan association, or bank, loans you money on the property, it has a direct financial interest in helping you guard yourself on certain points, such as making sure that there are no old mortgages, no unpaid back taxes, or bills for building materials, or other claims against the property.

Be certain your title is clear, or have it insured or guaranteed. Learn of any easements, such as the right of a telephone company to place its poles upon your lot.

If you make a purchase offer with a cash deposit, include a statement as to whether window shades, stoves, and other movable property are included. Risk from loss by fire or elements should be assumed by the owner until the title passes to you.

Your offer should be dependent on your obtaining a satisfactory loan to finance the proposition, and the ability of the owners to furnish papers to show a good marketable title, free from liens or encumbrances. In other words, do not bind yourself to the purchase until you are sure of what you are paying for, and that you can finance it.

You must be prepared to pay taxes on your property, and special assessments for installation of water, sewerage, electric light, gas or other public utilities, or street paving and sidewalks. Note what improvements are already made, and what additional ones you may have to pay for.

2.—HOW TO PAY FOR YOUR HOME

In buying a house and lot you must borrow what you cannot pay in cash. Remember that the more risks you assume, the fewer the lender will have to charge you for. Your promise to pay back what you borrow will be secured by a mortgage or trust on the property. A first mortgage loan on not over one-half or two-thirds of the value of a piece of property is a very safe investment, and the rates of interest should be low. The lender on a second mortgage takes more risk, and rates of interest and discounts are higher. If you agree to buy a home without the title passing to you at once, the seller takes less risk, and you may save money.

3.—WHERE TO GET LOANS

There are building and loan associations throughout the country, usually organized to serve the needs of people like yourself, who wish to finance a home. Their plan of weekly or monthly payments, both on principal and for interest, has proved sound from the experience of millions of people as an aid to systematic saving. Loans may often be obtained from savings banks, trust companies, state banks, individuals, and trustees for estates.

Obtaining money on a second mortgage is usually not so easy. Remember that when the owner of a house takes a second mortgage in payment he may plan to sell it for four-fifths or less of its face value, and that he probably charges you accordingly.

Above all, when you start to save for a home do not throw your money into glittering schemes that promise big dividends and the chance to borrow money at 3 per cent or less. The concerns behind such schemes cannot be trusted.

4.—HOW MUCH CAN YOU AFFORD?

It is said that a man may own a home worth one and one-half to two and one-half times his annual income but the payments you make during the first few years after purchasing are what you should pay most attention to. Rent ordinarily requires from ten per cent, to twenty-five, or even more, of a family's annual income. In addition to what you ordinarily pay for rent, you can devote your customary savings, or more, to paying off the principal of loans on your home.

Following is an example: A man who earns $2,000 a year buys a house and lot costing $4,000. He has $1,000 cash to pay down on it, and obtains a loan of $3,000, or 75 per cent, of the value of the property, from a building and loan association.

Cost per year for a $4,000 house (not including depreciation)

Payments on $3,000 B. & L. Shares at

½% a month or 6% a year (savings)	$180.00	a year
Interest on $3,000 loan at 6%	180.00	a year
Interest on $1,000 cash at 5%	50.00	a year
Taxes (vary locally)	75.00	a year
Insurance	5.00	a year
Upkeep at 1½%	60.00	a year
	$550.00	

Of the total income of $2,000, the $550 represents 27½% divided as follows: 18½% for rent; 9% for savings. In about twelve years the loan is paid off, and the home owned free and clear.

ZONING AND WHAT IT MEANS
TO THE HOME

BY DR. JOHN M. GRIES

CHIEF DIVISION OF BUILDING AND HOUSING,
DEPARTMENT OF COMMERCE

Zoning helps home owners by establishing residential districts from which garages, and business and factory buildings are excluded. Apartments or houses covering more than 30 or 40 per cent. of the area of a lot may be prohibited in some sections. This all means a better and fairer chance for each family to have a home with enough light and air, and healthful, decent surroundings, near to schools, playgrounds and transportation facilities.

It may be added that zoning, when wisely carried out, provides for grouping of neighborhood stores at convenient points, and for guided growth of business and industrial districts, in the directions best suited for them.

In the words of the Advisory Committee on Zoning appointed by Secretary Hoover:

"Zoning is the application of common sense and fairness to the public regulations governing the use of private real estate. It is a painstaking, honest effort to provide each district or neighborhood, as nearly as practicable, with just such protection and just such liberty as are sensible in that particular district. It avoids the error of trying to apply exactly the same building regulations to every part of a city or town regardless of whether it is a suburban residence section or a factory district, or a business and financial center.

"Zoning gives everyone who lives or does business in a community a chance for the reasonable enjoyment of his rights. At the same time it protects him from unreasonable injury by neighbors who would seek private gain at his expense.

"Zoning regulations differ in different districts according to the determined uses of the land for residence, business, or manufacturing, and according to the advisable heights and ground areas.

"But these differing regulations are the same for all districts of the same type. They treat all men alike."

But the benefits of zoning are not confined to safeguarding the home and its surroundings. It can reduce losses due to topsy-turvy growth of cities, and cut the cost of living. Every year millions of dollars are wasted in American cities from the scrapping of buildings in "blighted" districts. For instance, fine residential districts may be threatened by sporadic factories or junk yards, and owners may become panicky and sell at a sacrifice millions of dollars worth of valuable dwellings which will be left to stand practically idle. The public must pay for this loss in one way or another. Frequently money for street, sewers and other utilities need never be spent if it is known in advance that large factories are to occupy new developments. Industry and homes are both more efficient if kept generally separate, though separation need not mean great distances for workers to travel.

"How has zoning worked?" "What has it accomplished?" About 70 cities and towns have adopted zoning ordinances since 1916, and the idea has worked well. Reliable authorities declare that "the New York zoning regulations have prevented vast depreciation in many districts and effected savings in values amounting to millions of dollars in established sections." The highest class residential districts in New York, in which only 30 per cent of the lot area may be used for dwellings, have developed with much greater confidence, due to the knowledge that houses built would be safe from invasion by apartments or industry.

In St. Louis "it was found that residences tended to follow the residence districts, and did not even attempt to seek locations in industrial or unrestricted areas. Except commercial buildings which were built partly in commercial and partly in industrial districts, the development of St. Louis is said to be fitting itself very closely to the zoning plan.

"In New Jersey it has been found that the unzoned suburban town is at a distinct disadvantage as compared with the community protected by a zoning ordinance."

It is sometimes said that zoning is arbitrary and restricts the liberty of the individual to do as he wishes; but when zoning laws have been sensibly and comprehensively drawn, the courts have approved them as a reasonable exercise of the police power "for the public health, safety and general welfare."

Zoning should always be undertaken in close relation to a city plan. It is essentially a neighborly proposition, and there should be neighborhood meetings to explain it and gather suggestions.

The purpose of a zoning ordinance is to insure that growth, instead of taking place sporadically and wastefully, should go on in an orderly way in response to generally recognized needs, and with due notice to all concerned.

Zoning today is giving security and the sense of security to hundreds of thousands of families in America, in the enjoyment of happy homes amid the right kind of surroundings.

Is your city zoned?

Lector House believes that a society develops through a two-fold approach of continuous learning and adaptation, which is derived from the study of classic literary works spread across the historic timeline of literature records. Therefore, we aim at reviving, repairing and redeveloping all those inaccessible or damaged but historically as well as culturally important literature across subjects so that the future generations may have an opportunity to study and learn from past works to embark upon a journey of creating a better future.

This book is a result of an effort made by Lector House towards making a contribution to the preservation and repair of original ancient works which might hold historical significance to the approach of continuous learning across subjects.

HAPPY READING & LEARNING!

LECTOR HOUSE LLP
E-MAIL: lectorpublishing@gmail.com